I0464606

U.S. Department of Justice
Office of Justice Programs
National Institute of Justice

National Institute of Justice

Law Enforcement and Corrections Standards and Testing Program

Guide for the Selection of Communication Equipment for Emergency First Responders

NIJ Guide 104–00

Volume I
February 2002

U.S. Department of Justice
Office of Justice Programs
810 Seventh Street N.W.
Washington, DC 20531

John Ashcroft
Attorney General

Deborah J. Daniels
Assistant Attorney General

Sarah V. Hart
Director, National Institute of Justice

For grant and funding information, contact:
Department of Justice Response Center
800–421–6770

Office of Justice Programs
World Wide Web Site
http://www.ojp.usdoj.gov

National Institute of Justice
World Wide Web Site
http://www.ojp.usdoj.gov/nij

U.S. Department of Justice
Office of Justice Programs
National Institute of Justice

Guide for the Selection of Communication Equipment for Emergency First Responders

NIJ Guide 104–00, Volume I

Dr. Alim A. Fatah[1]
John A. Barrett[2]
Richard D. Arcilesi, Jr.[2]
Dr. Patrick S. Scolla[2]
Charlotte H. Lattin[2]
Susan D. Fortner[2]

Coordination by:
Office of Law Enforcement Standards
National Institute of Standards and Technology
Gaithersburg, MD 20899–8102

Prepared for:
National Institute of Justice
Office of Science and Technology
Washington, DC 20531

February 2002

NCJ 191160

---

[1] National Institute of Standards and Technology, Office of Law Enforcement Standards.

[2] Battelle Memorial Institute.

National Institute of Justice

Sarah V. Hart
Director

This guide was prepared for the National Institute of Justice, U.S. Department of Justice, by the Office of Law Enforcement Standards of the National Institute of Standards and Technology under Interagency Agreement 94–IJ–R–004, Project No. 99–060–CBW. It was also prepared under CBIAC contract No. SPO–900–94–D–0002 and Interagency Agreement M92361 between NIST and the Department of Defense Technical Information Center (DTIC).

The authors wish to thank Ms. Kathleen Higgins of the National Institute of Standards and Technology, Mr. Bill Haskell of SBCCOM, Ms. Priscilla S. Golden of General Physics, LTC Don Buley of the Joint Program Office of Biological Defense, Ms. Nicole Trudel of Camber Corporation, Dr. Stephen Morse of Centers for Disease Control, and Mr. Todd Brethauer of the Technical Support Working Group for their significant contributions to this effort. We would also like to acknowledge the Interagency Board for Equipment Standardization and Interoperability, which consists of Government and first responder representatives.

FOREWORD

The Office of Law Enforcement Standards (OLES) of the National Institute of Standards and Technology (NIST) furnishes technical support to the National Institute of Justice (NIJ) program to support law enforcement and criminal justice in the United States. OLES's function is to develop standards and conduct research that will assist law enforcement and criminal justice agencies in the selection and procurement of quality equipment.

OLES is: (1) subjecting existing equipment to laboratory testing and evaluation, and (2) conducting research leading to the development of several series of documents, including national standards, user guides, and technical reports.

This document covers research conducted by OLES under the sponsorship of NIJ. Additional reports as well as other documents are being issued under the OLES program in the areas of protective clothing and equipment, communication systems, emergency equipment, investigative aids, security systems, vehicles, weapons, and analytical techniques and standard reference materials used by the forensic community.

Technical comments and suggestions concerning this guide are invited from all interested parties. They may be addressed to the Office of Law Enforcement Standards, National Institute of Standards and Technology, 100 Bureau Drive, Stop 8102, Gaithersburg, MD 20899–8102.

Sarah V. Hart, Director
National Institute of Justice

CONTENTS

TABLES

FIGURES

COMMONLY USED SYMBOLS AND ABBREVIATIONS

A	ampere	h	hour	oz	ounce
ac	alternating current	hf	high frequency	o.d.	outside diameter
AM	amplitude modulation	Hz	hertz	Ω	ohm
cd	candela	i.d.	inside diameter	p.	page
cm	centimeter	in	inch	Pa	pascal
CP	chemically pure	IR	infrared	pe	probable error
c/s	cycle per second	J	joule	pp.	pages
d	day	L	lambert	ppm	parts per million
dB	decibel	L	liter	qt	quart
dc	direct current	lb	pound	rad	radian
°C	degree Celsius	lbf	pound-force	rh	relative humidity
°F	degree Fahrenheit	lbf·in	pound-force inch	s	second
dia	diameter	lm	lumen	SD	standard deviation
emf	electromotive force	ln	logarithm (base e)	sec.	Section
eq	equation	log	logarithm (base 10)	SWR	standing wave ratio
F	farad	M	molar	uhf	ultrahigh frequency
fc	footcandle	m	meter	UV	ultraviolet
fig.	Figure	μ	micron	V	volt
FM	frequency modulation	min	minute	vhf	very high frequency
ft	foot	mm	millimeter	W	watt
ft/s	foot per second	mph	miles per hour	N	newton
g	acceleration	m/s	meter per second	λ	wavelength
g	gram	mo	month	wk	week
gal	gallon	N·m	newton meter	wt	weight
gr	grain	nm	nanometer	yr	year
H	henry	No.	number		

area=unit^2 (e.g., ft^2, in^2, etc.); volume=unit^3 (e.g., ft^3, m^3, etc.)

ACRONYMS SPECIFIC TO THIS DOCUMENT

APCO	Association of Public Safety Communications Officials	MHz	Megahertz
CB	Citizens Band	PCS	Personal Communication System
CTCSS	Continuous Tone Coded Squelch System	PMR	Private Mobile Radio
DCS	Digital Code Squelch	PTT	Push-to-Talk
EDACS	Enhanced Digital Access Communications Systems	RF	Radio Frequency
GHz	Gigahertz	SMR	Shared Mobile Radio
I.S.	Intrinsically Safe	TETRA	Terrestrial Trunked Radio
LMR	Land Mobile Radios	VOX	Voice Operated Switch
LTR	Logic Trunked Radio		

DEFINITIONS RELEVENT TO THIS DOCUMENT

CDMA	Code Division Multiple Access is a method of subdividing a band to permit access to the same frequency for multiple users.
TMDA	Time Division Multiple Access is a method of subdividing a band to permit access to the same frequency for multiple users.
ISM Bands	Nonlicensed/nonexclusive frequency bands for Industrial, Scientific, and Medical applications. Frequency bands (902 MHz to 928 MHz, 2.40 GHz to 2.483 GHz) set aside for low-power devices (also referred to as "Part 15" devices).
DSSS	Direct Sequence and Spread Spectrum (an RF transmission scheme to permit multiple, coordinated users to operate in the same band).
FHSS	Frequency Hopping and Spread Spectrum (an RF transmission scheme to permit multiple, coordinated users to operate in the same band).
PASS	Personal alarm system, or warning device, worn by individuals.
Duplex	Real or perceived simultaneous transmit and receive.
Half-duplex	Continuous receive of all transmitted information and a transmit frequency/time slot/code shared with others.

PREFIXES (See ASTM E380)

d	deci (10^{-1})	da	deka (10)
c	centi (10^{-2})	h	hecto (10^2)
m	milli (10^{-3})	k	kilo (10^3)
μ	micro (10^{-6})	M	mega (10^6)
n	nano (10^{-9})	G	giga (10^9)
p	pico (10^{-12})	T	tera (10^{12})

COMMON CONVERSIONS

0.30480 m = 1 ft	4.448222 N = 1 lbf
25.4 mm = 1 in	1.355818 J = 1 ft·lbf
0.4535924 kg = 1 lb	0.1129848 N m = 1 lbf·in
0.06479891g = 1gr	14.59390 N/m = 1 lbf/ft
0.9463529 L = 1 qt	6894.757 Pa = 1 lbf/in^2
3600000 J = 1 kW·hr	1.609344 km/h = 1 mph

psi = mm of Hg x (1.9339×10^{-2})

mm of Hg = psi x 51.71

Temperature: $T_C = (T_F - 32) \times 5/9$ Temperature: $T_F = (T_C \times 9/5) + 32$

ABOUT THIS GUIDE

The National Institute of Justice is the focal point for providing support to State and local law enforcement agencies in the development of counterterrorism technology and standards, including technological needs for chemical and biological defense. In recognizing the needs of State and local emergency first responders, the Office of Law Enforcement Standards (OLES) at the National Institute of Standards and Technology (NIST), supported by the National Institute of Justice (NIJ), the Technical Support Working Group (TSWG), the U.S. Army Soldier and Biological Chemical Command, and the Interagency Board for Equipment Standardization and Interoperability (IAB), is developing chemical and biological defense equipment guides. These guides will focus on chemical and biological equipment in areas of detection, personal protection, decontamination, and communication. This guide focuses specifically on communication equipment and was developed to assist the emergency first responder community in the evaluation and purchase of communication equipment that can be used in conjunction with chemical and biological protective clothing and respiratory equipment.

The long range plans include these goals: (1) subject existing communication equipment to laboratory testing and evaluation against a specified protocol, and (2) conduct research leading to the development of a series of documents, including national standards, user guides, and technical reports. It is anticipated that the testing, evaluation, and research processes will take several years to complete; therefore, the National Institute of Justice has developed this initial guide for the emergency first responder community to facilitate their evaluation and purchase of communication equipment.

In conjunction with this program, additional guides, as well as other documents, are being issued in the areas of chemical agent and toxic industrial material detection equipment, biological agent detection equipment, decontamination equipment, and personal protective equipment.

The information contained in this guide has been obtained primarily through literature searches and market surveys. The vendors were contacted during the preparation of this guide to ensure data accuracy. In addition, the information contains test data obtained from other sources (e.g., Department of Defense) if available. It should be noted that the purpose of this guide is not to make recommendations about which equipment should be purchased, but to provide to the reader with information available from vendors so commercially available equipment can be compared and contrasted. *Reference herein to any specific commercial products, processes, or services by trade name, trademark, manufacturer, or otherwise does not necessarily constitute or imply its endorsement, recommendation, or favoring by the United States Government. The information and statements contained in this guide shall not be used for the purposes of advertising, nor to imply the endorsement or recommendation of the United States Government.*

With respect to information provided in this guide, neither the United States Government nor any of its employees make any warranty, expressed or implied, including but not limited to the warranties of merchantability and fitness for a particular purpose. Further, neither the United States Government nor any of its employees assume any legal liability or responsibility for the accuracy, completeness, or usefulness of any information, apparatus, product or process disclosed.

Technical comments, suggestions, and product updates are encouraged from interested parties. They may be addressed to the Office of Law Enforcement Standards, National Institute of Standards and Technology, 100 Bureau Drive, Stop 8102, Gaithersburg, MD 20899–8102. It is anticipated that this guide will be updated periodically.

Questions relating to the specific devices included in this document should be addressed directly to the proponent agencies or the equipment manufacturers. Contact information for each equipment item included in this guide can be found in Volume II.

1. INTRODUCTION

This guide includes information that is intended to assist the emergency first responder community in the evaluation and purchase of communication equipment that can be used in conjunction with chemical and biological protective clothing and respiratory equipment. It includes a market survey of communication technologies and commercially available equipment known to the authors as of February 2001. Brief technical discussions are presented that consider the principles of operation of several pieces of equipment. These may be ignored by readers who find them too technical, while those wanting additional information can obtain it from the list of references that is included in appendix B.

The primary purpose of this guide is to provide emergency first responders with information that should aid them in the evaluation and purchase of communication equipment that can be used in conjunction with chemical and biological protective clothing and respiratory equipment. The guide is more practical than technical and provides information on a variety of factors that can be considered when purchasing communication equipment, including secure communications compatibility, line of sight (how far transmission can travel), and digital communications compatibility, to name a few.

Due to the large number of communication equipment items identified in this guide, the guide is separated into two volumes. Volume I represents the actual guide, and Volume II serves as a supplement to Volume I since it contains the communication equipment data sheets only.

Readers who find this material too technical can omit this information while still making use of the rest of the guide, and readers who desire more technical detail can obtain it from the references listed in appendix B and the data sheets provided in Volume II. Volume I is divided into several sections. Section 2 provides an overview of communication systems. Specifically, it discusses system technologies, equipment types, accessories, and enhancements. Section 3 discusses various characteristics and performance parameters that are used to evaluate communication equipment in this guide. These characteristics and performance parameters are referred to as selection factors in the remainder of this guide. Fourteen selection factors have been identified. These factors were compiled by a panel of scientists and engineers who have multiple years of experience with communication equipment, domestic preparedness, and identification of emergency first responder needs. The factors have also been shared with the emergency responder community to get their thoughts and comments. Section 4 presents several tables that allow the reader to use the 14 selection factors to compare and contrast the different communication equipment.

Three appendices are also included within this guide. Appendix A lists questions that could assist emergency first responders when selecting communication equipment. Appendix B lists the documents that were referenced in this guide. Appendix C contains information about communication equipment safety.

2. OVERVIEW OF COMMUNICATION SYSTEMS

A communication system is made up of devices that employ one of two communication methods (wireless or wired), different types of equipment (portable radios, mobile radios, base/fixed station radios, and repeaters), and various accessories (examples include speaker microphones, battery eliminators, and carrying cases) and/or enhancements (encryption, digital communications, security measures, and interoperability/networking) to meet the user needs. This section provides the reader with information on the system technologies and the system enhancements. The technologies are discussed in section 2.1, types of equipment are presented in section 2.2, accessories are discussed in section 2.3, and enhancements are discussed in section 2.4.

2.1 Technologies

For practical purposes, a communication system can be considered to be "wired" or "wireless" (e.g., conventional telephone, radio communications, etc.). A wired system is technically known as a hard-line system and can be thought of as a localized, private telephone system that uses wires to operate over a limited area. A wireless system uses radio frequencies to "connect" users and is capable of operating over a much larger geographical area than a hard-line (wired) system. Since the communication equipment available to emergency first responders today does not use optical transmission methods, only radio frequency (RF) equipment will be considered here.

The major advantages of RF communication systems over hard-line communication systems are their ability to provide communications over large distances, through some obstacles (depending on the frequency), and to an almost unlimited number of users. The range of the signal is defined to be the distance between the transmitter and the receiver at which the amplitude of the signal received by the receiver is less than the amplitude of the background noise. For example, a person can experience this noise using low-cost "walkie-talkies." When the separation between the two walkie-talkies is great enough, the voice signal is lost and all that is heard is the background noise (sometimes called static). The range of the signal in a communication system may also be affected by interference from atmospheric disturbances, such as electrical storms, and high-power RF sources (such as radar equipment and broadcast equipment). Also, RF signals do not pass through water. Radio transmission quality also begins to deteriorate as the edge of the coverage area is approached.

Shared communication systems such as radios, the Internet, and telephone conference calls are subject to saturation by users (the maximum capacity whereby adding users will deteriorate and degrade the amount and quality of information able to be transferred over the system), a problem that compounds exponentially as the number of users increases. Communication system efficiency requires that the users follow published communication system guidelines regarding proper system discipline in order to ensure maximum efficiency of communication traffic.

2.1.1 Radio Frequency

Wireless systems (radios) transmit data and voice information using a specific radio frequency (RF) to other radios tuned to the same frequency. Common radio messages are transmitted over the RF band between 0.05 MHz and 900 MHz. Most public safety communications radios (portable, mobile, base station, and repeaters) transmit frequencies between 30 MHz and 900 MHz which are dedicated to public service use. Cell phones and systems, such as global positioning receivers, call boxes, electronic signs, irrigation systems, and mobile command units, that transmit information from remote locations, transmit in the microwave band between 1 GHz and 20 GHz. An example of RF technology that transmits only data is the SD–125 RF Link Module, manufactured by Maxon, shown in figure 2–1.

Figure 2–1. SD-125 RF
link module, Maxon

2.1.1.1 Conventional Radio System

In conventional RF systems, each user group is assigned a discrete radio channel (or frequency) that is independent of other user group channels (or frequencies). The users within the group transmit and receive only on that channel, on a first come first serve basis. Transmissions may occur with or without the assistance of a repeater (see sec. 2.2.4). Communications without a repeater are considered to be simplex communications (transmit and receive on the same frequency) and are typically used when only a small coverage area is required.

Conventional radio systems provide communication between users within a given geographic coverage area. A major advantage of a conventional radio system is that users equipped with radios from different manufacturers can communicate with one another provided they are programmed to the same frequency, which includes the appropriate CTCSS or DCS programming. (CTCSS and DCS are techniques commonly employed to aid in the rejection of interference from other radio systems). Disadvantages to conventional radio systems include user accessibility delays when a channel is being utilized by other users, and security concerns because of the ease of "eavesdropping" on potentially sensitive communications by the public or

4

media equipped with scanner radios. Modulation and encryption system compatibility must also be addressed in planning for interoperable communications. Figures 2–2 and 2–3 illustrate a mobile and a portable conventional radio, respectively. The mobile radio is a Kenwood Compact Synthesized FM Mobile Radio, TK-862H, and the portable radio is a Relm GPH21.

Figure 2–2. TK-862H, compact synthesized
FM mobile radio, Kenwood

Figure 2–3. GPH21,
portable radio, Relm

2.1.1.2 Trunked Radio Systems

Trunked radio systems typically allocate 20 or more talk groups (logical channels) to a particular radio frequency channel. A radio system's computer assigns a user and the user group to a frequency when the push-to-talk (PTT) button is pressed. A user is an officer or member assigned to the precinct or fire company, and a user group is a police precinct or fire company. This results in a single conversation occurring over several channels, eliminating the need for the users to manually change frequencies, thus maximizing the system efficiency. In addition, the channel capacity increases because other users can use the time between transmissions for their communications without the need to wait for a "clear channel." Because the computer selects the channel and monitors the repeater before transmitting, the trunked radio system is more technically complex than the conventional system. Since it appears to be simpler and faster to use, it may be considered more efficient. Another apparent advantage to a trunked system is the increased difficulty in eavesdropping on conversations that may switch channels with every transmission. However, scanners that can follow talk groups on a trunked radio system are widely available to the general public, whereby digital spread spectrum radios may provide user security from such methods of eavesdropping.

The disadvantages of the trunked system are those common to all RF radio systems (i.e., atmospheric interference, unreliability in certain environments, such as underground and confined spaces, and unable to be used in explosive environments, etc.). Additional disadvantages of the trunked system include the increased complexity of the infrastructure with

5

regards to an increased number of antenna and repeater sites (especially in the case of 800 MHz systems), dependence on the computer system and software that controls the trunked system, and reliance on the equipment of one manufacturer for guaranteed operation. Examples of trunked radios are shown in figures 2–4 and 2–5. Figure 2–4 is a Yaesu/Vertex-Standard GX 4800UT UHF mobile radio, and figure 2–5 is a portable system, the Yaesu/Vertex-Standard HX482UT conventional and trunked system.

Figure 2–4. GX 4800UT UHF trunked system mobile radio, Yaesu/Vertex-Standard

Figure 2–5. HX482UT, conventional and trunked system, Yaesu/Vertex-Standard

2.1.2 Hard-Line Technology

Hard-line communication systems operate by transmitting voice and data through a cable that connects to a telephone-like apparatus. The major advantage of a hard-line system is the ability to communicate from underground, confined spaces, shielded enclosures, collapsed structure void spaces, and similar locations (such as explosive environments) where RF systems are unreliable or unable to be used. An additional advantage of hard-line communication systems is that they are totally secure. Outside eavesdropping is not possible because the transmissions are contained within the wired system. The disadvantages of a hard-line system are the distance and mobility constraints imposed by the cable, the time required to set the system up at an incident site, and the limited number of users that can be supported by a system at a given location.

2.2 Types of Equipment

The RF communication equipment considered in this guide includes portable radios, mobile radios, base/fixed station radios, repeaters, and base station/repeaters. Each type of equipment will be discussed in the following sections.

2.2.1 Portable Radios

Portable radios are small, lightweight, handheld, wireless communication units that contain both a transmitter and a receiver, a self-contained microphone and speaker, an attached power supply (typically a rechargeable battery), and antenna. Portable transceivers (such as a walkie-talkie) have relatively low-powered transmitters (1 W to 5 W), need to have their batteries periodically recharged or replaced, and may be combined in a wireless radio communication system with other portable, mobile, and base station radios. There are also very low-powered transceivers, available with power outputs of 0.1 W, which are generally linked to portable repeaters for extended range and interoperability with higher-powered radio systems.

2.2.2 Mobile Radios

Mobile radios are larger than portable radios and are designed to be mounted in a fixed location inside a vehicle (police cruiser, fire truck, etc.). Like the portable radios, mobile radios contain both a transmitter and a receiver and may contain an internal speaker. However, mobile radios connect to the vehicle's power supply, which enables them to have a higher transmitter output power (typically 5 W to 50 W) and an external antenna. The microphone is usually handheld, and the speaker may be externally located to the radio. Because of the higher transmitter power and external antenna, the effective communication range is greater than that of a portable radio, especially if a repeater is not used. The receivers in mobile radios are generally more sensitive than the receivers found in portable radios, as physical space for components in mobile radios is not as critical as in portable radios. Personnel who do not need to communicate with others when away from the vehicle typically use mobile radios. As with portable radios, mobile radios may be combined into a radio communication system with other portable, mobile, and base station radios.

2.2.3 Base/Fixed Station Radios

A base (or fixed) station radio also contains a transmitter and a receiver. The radio is powered by an external electrical system (typically 110 V ac) and is connected to an antenna located tens to hundreds of feet away, typically on top of a building or on a tower. Because the base station radio uses an external electrical system (i.e., commercial power mains), compared with portable and mobile radios, they have the most powerful transmitters (5 W to hundreds of watts) and the most sensitive receivers. Microphones can either be handheld or desktop models, and the speaker can either be external or internal to the radio.

2.2.4 Repeaters

A repeater is a specialized radio that contains both a receiver and a transmitter. Repeaters are used to increase the effective communications coverage area for portable, mobile, or base station radios that otherwise might not be able to communicate with one another. The repeater's receiver is tuned to the frequency used by a portable, mobile, or base station transmitter for incoming signals, and the repeater's transmitter is tuned to the frequency used by a portable, mobile, or base station receiver. The incoming signal is rebroadcast back to the radio network on a different frequency, usually with higher power and from a better location (tall buildings, mountaintops, and/or towers). Figure 2–6 shows a Vertex VXR-5000 repeater.

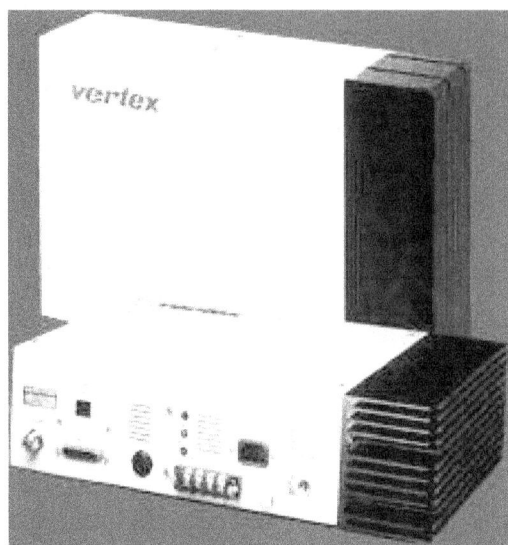

Figure 2–6. VXR-5000 repeater, Vertex

2.2.5 Base Station/Repeaters

Several manufacturers offer base station/repeater radios. These radios cannot operate as both a base station and a repeater simultaneously, but when installed for use, they are configured to operate as either a base station or as a repeater.

2.3 Accessories

Most accessories are for portable radios and are designed to allow for maximum user flexibility. There are optional trunking accessory boards available for many conventional radio systems, and optional encryption modules available for some radios to allow for secure communications.

2.3.1 Accessories for Portable Radios

Additional accessories for portable radios include optional batteries for extended operating time, speaker-microphones, carrying cases, battery eliminators, and vehicular adapters. Multiple carrying case options are available: those that allow for optional batteries; those that have specialized operations mounting requirements, such as the strap-on chest case for instances when a radio cannot be worn on or near the waist; or those that are water resistant for operations that may occur in extremely wet environments.

Several optional speaker-microphones attach to portable radios through the remote speaker/microphone jack. These include boom microphones (attenuates background noise and works best when the user's voice is not obstructed), ear microphones (worn in the ear and transmits ear canal vibrations into microphone signals), bone microphones (worn on the top of the head or behind the ear and transmits vibration signals), and throat microphones (worn on the throat and transmits vibration signals). Voice operated switch (VOX) activated accessories have the same function as the PTT button but allow hands-free use of the radio. Alternately, full duplex operation of radios (able to transmit and receive on different frequencies simultaneously) provides hands-free and simultaneous, bi-directional communications.

Battery eliminators are specialized accessories that are attached to the radio in place of the battery. They allow portable radios to operate from a power source such as the electrical system of the vehicle rather than the radio's own battery, thus extending the useable life of the radio's battery before it needs to be recharged. Battery eliminators are most often used with portable radios that have no external power (e.g., 12 V dc) jack. Battery eliminators can be obtained from radio manufacturers or specialized third party aftermarket vendors.

Vehicular adapters are also specialized adapters for portable radios that allow portable radios to operate as a mobile radio. When the portable radio is placed into a vehicular adapter, the radio operates off the electrical system of the vehicle, is connected to an antenna mounted on the vehicle, and in some instances, is connected to an amplifier in order to increase the output power of the transmitter (for example, 5 W to 50 W for increased range). While the portable radio is in the vehicular adapter, the radio's battery is recharged.

2.3.2 Accessories for Mobile Radios and Base Station/Repeater Radios

There are fewer accessories available for mobile and base station radios. They are generally chosen when the radio is initially purchased because they are often dependent upon installation requirements and restrictions.

Accessories for mobile and base station radios typically include these devices: transmitter power amplifiers, specialized modules that allow the radio to be connected to computers or other data terminals, remote mounting systems to minimize theft, external speakers that can be mounted for operator convenience, and specialized microphones that may allow for the user to change channels or transmitter output power.

2.4 Enhancements

Enhancements are those items or applications available to the customer for modification of the communication system for a specific purpose. Enhancements discussed in this section include the following items: encryption, digital communications, security measures, and interoperability/networking.

2.4.1 Encryption

Both conventional and trunked RF radios may allow for the encryption of sensitive communications for security purposes if the system is equipped with the appropriate encryption electronics. Some radios may require the installation of an optional encryption module for secure communications. Voice and data transmissions may be encrypted by simple inversion, rolling code, or by digital encryption. Protection from scanner monitoring and even more sophisticated monitoring devices can also be accomplished with spread spectrum radios operating in the ISM bands; however, because of the low power utilized in the ISM bands, reliable communications may not be possible.

2.4.2 Digital Communications

Digital communications is a technique whereby voice (sound waves) and data information present in the radio signals is converted into binary code represented using electronic or electromagnetic signals. The binary code is then converted by mathematical algorithms that need to be decoded by mathematical algorithms in the receiving radio in order for the user to understand the information. It offers users enhanced signaling and control options, more consistent audio quality, greater radio spectrum efficiency, and a broader range of encryption capabilities. Communications between users is less likely to be interrupted in terms of signals being dropped. At the edges of a coverage area, digital technology improves the signal integrity to maximize communications.

To help understand digital communications technology, it is important to understand analog communications technology. Analog communications is the transmission of information using a continuously variable electromagnetic signal. The information usually transmitted by analog systems is from sound, such as that contained in conversation and music. Prior to transmission of the sound information, it must be converted into an electrical form (as is done with a microphone). For several technical reasons, the electrical information is typically transformed into higher frequencies by modulating a continuous wave radio signal. Examples of this type of transformation and modulation are the FM and AM signals on your radio. Analog communications is the basis for most current cell phones and communication systems. Perhaps the best and simplest example of analog radio communications is the Citizens Band (CB) radio service.

2.4.3 Security Measures

Communications security is becoming increasingly important. Presently, the general public can purchase any one of several different radio receivers that will allow them to monitor virtually any and all public safety communications. As a result, secure communications may be difficult to achieve unless measures are incorporated into the planning of a communication system.

Security measures that can be incorporated into a communication system include, but are not limited to, digital encryption of radio signals, voice inversion, digitizing of voice and data as in a digital system, and use of digital cellular or PCS telephone circuits. Security may also be improved by the use of spread spectrum techniques. No single security measure is appropriate for every situation, nor is it necessarily true that all security technologies will work with, or are appropriate for, all communication systems. Encryption systems may require extensive planning and coordination to ensure compatibility and interoperability. It is best to consult with the radio manufacturer's sales and technical personnel for the most reliable and accurate information regarding current encryption technologies and their uses.

2.4.4 Interoperability and Networking

Interoperability is the process of connecting different groups using different radio systems and communication technologies (telephones, radios, cellular communications, and satellite communications) so that they can communicate directly with one another without having to go through multiple dispatchers or relay personnel. In the context of communications, interoperability describes the situation where different communication systems that are otherwise incompatible with one another work together without relying on the addition of considerably more manpower. An example of interoperability would be where a police radio system can "directly" exchange information (voice or data) with the National Guard radio system or the FEMA radio system; or a municipality's public works department using a Motorola Type I Trunked System can "directly" exchange information (voice or data) with the adjacent jurisdiction's fire department which uses a Com-Net Ericsson EDACS Trunked System. Some trunked radio systems may allow for interoperability between different talk groups and may allow the connection of third party dispatch systems. Integration with other communication systems may also be permitted. These systems may include private automatic branch exchange (PABX) systems, data networks, cordless extensions, and paging systems. Examples of data networks that a radio system may be interoperable with are automatic vehicle location and Geographic Positioning Satellite systems. Another example is a telephone interconnect system where telephone calls are patched through the radio system.

Simply stated, a communications interconnect system allows telephones, cell phones, radios on different frequencies, proprietary formats, trunked talk groups, and conventional radio networks to communicate with each other using interface modules. The interconnect system can allow for several two-way and conference calls to occur simultaneously. There is no need for a dispatcher to connect one system to another system as the cross-connection operations are unmanned. This can result in a much greater interoperability between equipment and organizations. Figure 2–7 is the JPS TRP-1000 Transportable Radio Interconnect System, and Figure 2–8 shows the Communications Applied Technology (C-AT) ICRI battery powered, man-carry radio interconnect "switch."

2.4.5 Incident Management and Assessment Tools

In developing the Chemical-Biological defense equipment guides, a number of incident management and assessment tools were identified that are available to the emergency first responder community. Several of these tools, as well as their internet addresses, are listed in the following paragraphs.

11

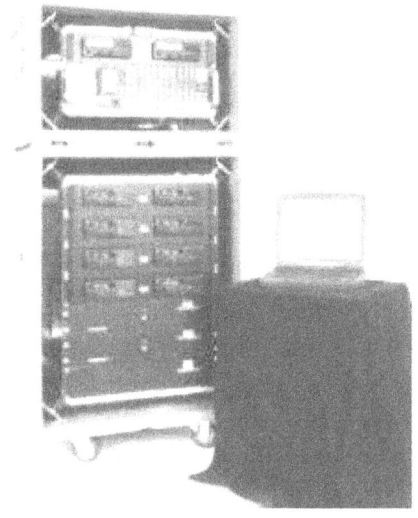

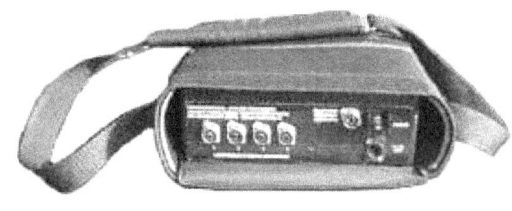

Figure 2–7. TRP-1000 transportable radio interconnect system, JPS

Figure 2–8. ICIR man-carry radio interconnect switch, C-AT

Consequence Assessment Tool (CATS) is a disaster analysis system for Natural and Technological Hazards that was developed for the Defense Threat Reduction Agency (DTRA) and the Federal Emergency Management Agency (FEMA). It is supplied with over 150 databases and map layers to help the emergency response organizations before (for training and planning), during (to assess quickly and accurately), and after (to obtain information and support) a disaster. It can be customized per user requirements. The internet address for CATS is http://cats.saic.com/main.html.

Chemical Biological Response Aide (COBRA) is an internet site that offers a family of products and services for the emergency first responder. The COBRA Guide 2000 is an interactive, electronic version of the Department of Transportation's (DOT) 2000 Emergency Response Guide book. The web site is www.defensegp.com/cobraproducts.cfm.

E Team is an internet-based workflow management application designed for emergency responders. This software is Incident Command System (ICS) compliant, allowing communication and data sharing between all command posts and operations centers. It is designed for incident reporting, resource request tracking, and infrastructure status reporting. The web site for E Team is http://www.eteam.com.

Each of the listed web sites has additional links to supplemental information for the emergency first responder.

3. COMMUNICATION EQUIPMENT SELECTION FACTORS

This section provides a discussion of 14 selection factors that are recommended for consideration by the emergency first responder community when selecting and purchasing communications equipment that can be used in conjunction with chemical and biological protective clothing and respiratory equipment. These factors were compiled by a panel of scientists and engineers who have multiple years of experience in communication equipment, domestic preparedness, emergency and public service communications, and identification of emergency first responder needs. The factors have also been shared with the emergency first responder community in order to get their thoughts and comments.

It is anticipated that, as additional input is received from the emergency first responder community, additional factors may be added or existing factors may be modified. These factors were developed so that communications equipment could be compared and contrasted in order to assist with the selection and purchase of the most appropriate equipment. *It is important to note that the evaluation conducted using the 14 selection factors was based solely upon vendor-supplied data and no independent evaluation of equipment was conducted in the development of this guide.* The vendor-supplied data can be found in its entirety in Volume II.

Prior to discussing each of the selection factors, it is important to note that although weight was considered an important selection factor for several of the other guides, weight was not included as a selection factor for communication equipment. By definition, a portable radio is light (< 2 lb), a mobile radio is attached to a vehicle (therefore weight is not critical), and repeaters are generally operated at a fixed location.

The results of the evaluation of the communication equipment against the 14 selection factors are provided in section 4. The remainder of this section defines each of the selection factors.

3.1 Maximum Transmitter Output Power

The transmitter output power refers to the maximum output power of the transmitter. For portable radios, too high an output power leads to a shortened battery use cycle (the time between battery recharging or replacing), or too low output can put the life of the responder operating the radio in jeopardy as the signal may not be able to be picked up by a repeater or another receiver.

The above limitations do not apply to mobile radios or repeaters since they have a higher output and an external power source.

3.2 Secure Communications Compatibility

Secure communications is the ability to encrypt and decrypt communications signals. Once properly encrypted, the communication equipment can transmit any signal.

3.3 Programmability

This selection factor defines how restrictive the radio programming is for the communications equipment. Programming communications equipment focuses primarily on the ability to add or delete channels. Depending on the equipment, the ability to program or reprogram a radio may be limited to authorized personnel and/or vendors. The equipment may be able to be programmed by the end user as well.

3.4 User Capability

User capability refers to the ability of the communication system to simultaneously support different types of users (e.g., fire, EMS, Command, and law enforcement). An "unlimited capability" refers to the ability of the equipment and/or system to support all users without any restrictions whatsoever. A "fixed capability" refers to a system that allows communications only within each group, with Command Officers, and with other groups via a "shared mutual aid" channel. "Restrictive capability" refers to a system that allows users to communicate only with others within their own user group and to Command Officers. A Command Officer can communicate with other Command Officers as well as all the user groups in the chain of command.

3.5 Line of Sight

Line of sight refers to the distance that transmissions can occur in a clear area (no obstructions such as skyscrapers, forests, etc.) without a repeater.

3.6 Power Requirements

Power requirements indicate whether specific equipment can operate on a battery and/or ac electrical power. Since power requirements are inherently different for portable and mobile/repeater equipment items, separate selection factors for these equipment items are presented.

3.7 Battery Life

Battery life is the ability of the portable radio equipped with an approved battery to operate at maximum transmitter power for an 8 h duty shift when used in a 5/5/90 operating mode (5 % of the time transmitting, 5 % of the time receiving with the squelch being broken, 90 % of the time receiving with the squelch not being broken—"standby"). To squelch is the ability to silence the radio in the absence of a desired incoming radio signal. This selection factor is only relevant for portable radios.

3.8 Battery Locking Ability

Battery locking ability considers how securely the battery is attached to the radio. This selection factor is only relevant for portable radios.

3.9 Vehicular Adapter (Portable Radios)

Vehicular adapter refers to whether the portable radio has an optional vehicular adapter accessory. The vehicular adapter accessory allows the portable radio to act like a mobile radio.

3.10 Digital Communications Compatibility

Digital communications compatibility refers to whether the radio is capable of digital communication with or without an adapter (a manufacturer or third party supplied module installed in the radio that permits operation on a digital communication system).

3.11 Durability

The durability of a piece of equipment describes the ruggedness of the equipment (i.e., can the equipment be dropped from several feet or submersed in water and still operate).

3.12 Unit Cost

Unit cost is the cost of the radio equipment, including the cost of all support equipment and consumables. This factor, in conjunction with other selection factors, can help the user decide if a radio will be deemed suitable for disposal after use, suitable for special uses only, or suitable for all uses.

3.13 Operator Skill Requirements

Operator skill level refers to the skill level and training required for the operation of the equipment.

3.14 Training Requirements

Training requirements are the amount of instruction time required for the operator to become proficient in the operation of the instrument. For example, higher-end equipment such as a repeater requires more in-depth training than a portable radio; therefore, this selection factor has different criteria for portable and mobile/repeater equipment items.

Details on the manner in which the selection factors were used to assess the equipment are presented in table 3–1.

Table 3-1. Selection factor key for communication equipment
February 2001

Selection Factor	●	◐	◑	○
Maximum Transmitter Power Output	Power output of 3 W to 6 W		Power output of more than 1.5 W but less than 3 W	Power output of less than 1.5 W
Secure Communications Compatibility	Capable of secure transmissions without an accessory	Capable of secure transmissions with an accessory	Not capable of secure transmissions	
Programmability	Can be programmed/reprogrammed by authorized personnel	Can be programmed/reprogrammed by vendor only	Can be programmed/reprogrammed by the end user	
User Capability	Unlimited capability		Fixed capability	Restrictive capability
Line of Sight	Transmission can travel 10 miles or more		Transmission can travel 5 miles to 10 miles	Transmission can travel less than 5 miles
Power Requirements (Portable)	Operates off battery pack, external dc or ac adapter	Operates off battery pack or external dc adapter	Operates off battery pack or ac adapter	Operates off battery pack only
Power Requirements (Mobile and Repeater)	Uses 12 V dc to 15 V ac		Uses 120/220 V ac	Uses voltage other than standard 12 V dc to 15 V dc or 110/220 V ac
Battery Life (Portable)	Equal to or greater than 8 h		Greater than 4 h but less than 8 h	Less than 4 h
Battery Locking Ability (Portable)	Battery securely locked into place on the radio and cannot be dislodged by bumping or dropping			Battery not locked into place
Vehicular Adapter (Portable)	Has vehicle adapter (with built-in amplifier) that connects to vehicle's electrical system and external antenna			Does not have optional vehicle adapter
Digital Communications Compatibility	Capable of digital transmissions without an adaptor		Capable of digital transmissions with an adaptor	Not capable of digital transmissions
Durability	Designed for rugged use and is submersible in water		Designed for rugged use but is not submersible in water	Designed for standard use only
Unit Cost	Less than or equal to $500 per unit		Greater than $500 but less than $1000 per unit	Greater than $1000 per unit
Operator Skill Level	No special skills or training required		No special skills but some training required	Technical background required to operate equipment
Training Requirements (Portable)	No special training required		Less than 60 min training required	More than 60 min training required
Training Requirements (Mobile and Repeater)	No special training required		Less than 8 h training required	More than 8 h training required

The gray cells designate that the symbol is not applicable for the selection factor.
A duplicate of this table is provided for quick reference (as Table 4-12).

4. COMMUNICATION EQUIPMENT EVALUATION

An extensive market survey was conducted to identify commercially available communication equipment. The market survey, which included the identification of new equipment and interaction with numerous equipment vendors, identified 181 different communication equipment items. Section 4, of this volume, documents the results of evaluating each equipment item versus the 14 selection factors identified in sec. 3. Section 4.1 defines the equipment usage categories and sec. 4.2 discusses the evaluation results. Volume II of this guide provides details of the market survey, as well as data on each piece of equipment.

4.1 Equipment Categories

To display the evaluation results in a meaningful format, the communication equipment was grouped into four categories primarily based on physical size and power requirements of the equipment. The following types of communication equipment in this guide are portable, mobile, base, and repeater.

- Portable equipment is small and self-contained transceivers (transmitter and receiver) that are easily carried by personnel.

- Mobile equipment is a transceiver that operates from the electrical supply of a vehicle and is typically connected to an external antenna.

- A base is a transceiver that typically operates from the electrical system of a building and is connected to an external antenna.

- A repeater is a radio that receives and retransmits signals from portable, mobile, and base radios to extend the range of all of the radios.

4.2 Evaluation Results

The evaluation results for the communication equipment are presented in tabular format for the 181 items of communication equipment that were identified at the time this guide was written. A table is presented for each equipment category (see sec. 4.1); the portable and mobile radios are further divided by their trunking capability. The rating of each item is indicated by a symbol: the open symbol indicates that the item does not meet the conditions of a specific selection factor, the partially filled circles indicate that the equipment partially meets the conditions of a selection factor, and the full circle indicates that the piece of equipment totally meets the conditions of a selection factor. The acronym "TBD" (to be determined) is displayed in the appropriate cell if data were not available to characterize a specific selection factor. The acronym "NA" is displayed in the appropriate cell if the data were not applicable for a piece of equipment. Table 4–1 provides the table number and associated table pages for each of the nine usage categories and the selection factor table.

Table 4–1. Evaluation results reference table

Table Name	Table Number	Page(s)
Portable (Conventional and Trunked)	4–3	20–25
Portable (Conventional)	4–4	26–30
Portable (Trunked)	4–5	31
Mobile (Conventional and Trunked)	4–6	32–35
Mobile (Conventional)	4–7	36–37
Mobile (Trunked)	4–8	38
Repeater	4–9	39–40
Base	4–10	41
Base Station and/or Repeater	4–11	42
Selection Factor Key for Communication Equipment	4–12	43

4.2.1 Portable

The results of categorizing the communication equipment are detailed in table 4–2. Radio equipment was further divided by the communication technology (see sec. 2.1) of each communication item.

There were 100 portable detectors identified in the development of this guide. These 100 portable radios were further divided into three subcategories identifying their trunking capability. There were 55 portable radios using the conventional technology (see sec. 2.1.1.1) that were also capable of trunking (with or without an accessory). There were 44 portable radios using the conventional technology only. There was one portable radio identified as using only the trunking technology (see sec. 2.1.1.2). Tables 4–3, 4–4, and 4–5 detail the evaluation results for all three of these subcategories, respectively.

4.2.2 Mobile

There were 54 mobile radios identified in the development of this guide. These 54 mobile radios were further divided into three subcategories identifying their trunking capability. There were 33 mobile radios using the conventional technology that were also capable of trunking (with or without an accessory). There were 19 mobile radios using the conventional technology only. There were two mobile radios identified as using only the trunking technology. Tables 4–6, 4–7, and 4–8 detail the evaluation results for all three of these subcategories, respectively.

4.2.3 Base Station/Repeaters

There were 27 base or repeater systems identified in the development of this guide. These 27 base or repeater systems were further divided into three subcategories (repeater, base station, or base station/repeater). There were 17 repeater systems, four base systems, and six base station/repeater systems.

4.2.3.1 Repeater

There were 17 repeater systems identified in the development of this guide. These 17 repeater systems were further divided into three subcategories identifying their trunking capability. There were four repeater systems using conventional technology that were also capable of trunking (with or without an accessory). There were 12 repeater systems using conventional technology. There was one repeater system identified as using only trunking technology. Table 4–9 details the evaluation results for the repeater communications equipment.

4.2.3.2 Base Station

There were four base stations identified in the development of this guide. All four of these systems used conventional technology. Table 4–10 details the evaluation results for the base stations.

4.2.3.3 Base Station/Repeater

There were six base/repeater systems identified in the development of this guide. These six repeater systems were further divided into three subcategories identifying their trunking capability. There were five systems using conventional technology that were also capable of trunking (with or without an accessory). There was one system using only conventional technology, and no systems using only trunking technology. Table 4–11 details the evaluation results for the repeater/base station equipment.

Table 4–2. Communication equipment technology format

Radio Type	Communication Format			
	Both	Conventional	Trunked	Total
Portable	55	44	1	100
Mobile	33	19	2	54
Repeater	4*	12*	1*	17
Base	0*	4*	0*	4
Base Station and/or Repeater	5*	1*	0*	6
Total	97	80	4	181

*Separate base, repeaters, and base/repeater tables were not created for conventional and trunked technologies.

Table 4-3. Portable communication equipment (conventional and trunked)
February 2001

Legend: ● = full, ◐ = half, ○ = empty

ID #	Equipment Name	Maximum Transmitter Power Output	Secure Communications Compatibility	Programmability	User Capability	Line of Sight	Power Requirements	Battery Life	Battery Locking Ability	Vehicular Adapter	Digital Communications Compatibility	Durability	Unit Cost	Operator Skill Level	Training Requirements
5	EDACS™ LPE-200™, Portable 800 MHz, 900 MHz	●	◐	●	●	○	●	●	●	◐	●	○	◐	◐	
9	ProVoice™ Jaguar™ 700P, 800 MHz	●	●	●	●	○	●	●	●	●	●	○	◐	◐	
10	ComNet Ericsson Jaguar Transceiver, Portable; Jaguar 700P, 800 MHz	●	●	●	●	○	●	●	TBD	◐	◐	○	◐	◐	
11	ComNet Ericsson M-RK™ Analog Portable, M-RK I	●	◐	●	●	○	●	●	●	◐	◐	◐	◐	◐	
12	ComNet Ericsson M-RK™ Analog Portable, M-RK II	●	◐	●	●	○	●	●	●	●	◐	○	◐	◐	
13	ComNet Ericsson M-RK™ Analog Portable, M-RK II Scan	●	●	●	●	○	●	●	●	◐	●	○	◐	◐	
23	ProVoice™ LPE-200™ Portable 800 MHz	●	●	●	●	○	●	●	●	●	●	○	◐	◐	
32	EFJohnson Transceiver, Portable; 77xx-800 MHz	◐	○	●	●	●	●	●	○	○	○	◐	◐	◐	
33	EFJohnson Transceiver, Portable; 98xx-800 MHz	●	○	●	●	●	NA	NA	NA	○	◐	◐	◐	◐	
34	EFJohnson Transceiver, Portable; 501x VHF	●	●	●	●	●	●	●	○	●	◐	○	◐	◐	

'TBD' (to be determined) - there is currently no data available to support that selection factor.
'NA' - data field is not applicable for this piece of equipment.
See Table 4-12 for selection factor definitions.

Table 4-3. Portable communication equipment (conventional and trunked)
February 2001

ID #	Equipment Name	Maximum Transmitter Power Output	Secure Communications Compatibility	Programmability	User Capability	Line of Sight	Power Requirements	Battery Life	Battery Locking Ability	Vehicular Adapter	Digital Communications Compatibility	Durability	Unit Cost	Operator Skill Level	Training Requirements
35	EF Johnson Transceiver, Portable; 504x UHF	●	●	●	TBD	●	●	●	○	●	◐	○	◐	◐	
36	EF Johnson Transceiver, Portable; 508x-800 MHz	◐	●	●	TBD	●	●	●	○	●	◐	○	◐	◐	
39	Icom VHF Transceiver, Portable; IC-F3	●	●	●	●	○	●	●	○	○	◐	●	●	●	
40	Icom VHF Transceiver, Portable; IC-F3S	●	○	●	●	○	●	●	○	○	◐	●	●	●	
41	Icom VHF Transceiver, Portable; IC-F3GT/ IC-F3GTS	●	◐	●	●	○	●	●	○	○	◐	●	●	●	
42	Icom UHF Transceiver, Portable; IC-F4	●	◐	●	○	○	●	●	○	○	◐	●	●	●	
43	Icom UHF Transceiver, Portable; IC-F4S	●	○	●	○	○	●	●	○	○	◐	●	●	●	
44	Icom UHF Transceiver, Portable; IC-F4GT/ IC-F4GTS	●	◐	●	●	○	●	●	○	○	◐	●	●	●	
49	Icom VHF Transceiver, Portable; IC-F30GS/ IC-F30GT	●	●	●	●	○	●	●	○	○	◐	◐	◐	◐	
50	Icom VHF Transceiver, Portable; IC-F30LT Land Use; IC-F30LT Marine Version	●	◐	●	●	○	●	●	○	○	●	◐	◐	◐	

[TBD (to be determined) - there is currently no data available to support that selection factor.
[NA - data field is not applicable for this piece of equipment.
See Table 4-12 for selection factor definitions.

21

Table 4-3. Portable communication equipment (conventional and trunked)
February 2001

ID #	Equipment Name	Maximum Transmitter Power Output	Secure Communications Compatibility	Programmability	User Capability	Line of Sight	Power Requirements	Battery Life	Battery Locking Ability	Vehicular Adapter	Digital Communications Compatibility	Durability	Unit Cost	Operator Skill Level	Training Requirements
51	Icom UHF Transceiver, Portable; IC-F40GS/ IC-F40GT	●	●	●	●	○	●	●	○	○	◐	◐	●	●	
52	Icom UHF Transceiver, Portable; IC-F40LT Land Use; IC-F40M/IC-F40LT Marine Version	●	◐	●	●	○	●	●	○	○	●	●	●	●	
55	Kenwood Synthesized FM Portable Radio; TK-260/G	●	○	●	○	○	●	●	●	◐	◐	●	◐	◐	
56	Kenwood Synthesized FM Portable Radio; TK-270/G	●	○	●	○	○	●	●	●	◐	◐	●	◐	◐	
57	Kenwood Synthesized FM Portable Radio; TK-360/G	●	○	●	○	○	●	●	●	○	◐	●	◐	◐	
58	Kenwood Synthesized FM Portable Radio; TK-370/G	●	○	●	○	○	●	●	●	○	◐	●	◐	◐	
80	Kenwood Synthesized FM Portable Radio/Trunked System; TK-280	●	◐	●	○	○	●	●	●	◐	◐	◐	◐	◐	
81	Kenwood Synthesized FM Portable Radio/Trunked System; TK-380	●	◐	●	○	○	●	●	●	◐	◐	◐	◐	◐	
82	Kenwood 800/900 MHz FM Transceiver, TK-480 and TK-480 NPSPAC	◐	◐	◐	○	○	●	●	●	◐	◐	◐	◐	◐	
84	Kenwood Trunked Portable Radios; TK-930HD/K2 NSPAC	●	◐	●	◐	●	NA	NA	NA	◐	◐	◐	◐	◐	

'NA' - data field is not applicable for this piece of equipment.
See Table 4-12 for selection factor definitions.

22

Table 4-3. Portable communication equipment (conventional and trunked)
February 2001

ID #	Equipment Name	Maximum Transmitter Power Output	Secure Communications Compatibility	Programmability	User Capability	Line of Sight	Power Requirements	Battery Life	Battery Locking Ability	Vehicular Adapter	Digital Communications Compatibility	Durability	Unit Cost	Operator Skill Level	Training Requirements
90	Motorola Astro Transceiver, Portable; Saber 1	●	◐	●	TBD	◔	TBD	TBD	●	●	○	○	◐	◐	
91	Motorola Astro Transceiver, Portable; Saber 2	●	◐	●	TBD	◔	TBD	TBD	●	◐	○	○	◐	◐	
92	Motorola Astro Transceiver, Portable; Saber 3	●	◐	●	TBD	◔	TBD	TBD	●	◐	○	○	◐	◐	
93	Motorola Astro Transceiver, Portable; XTS 3000 Model 1	●	◐	●	TBD	○	TBD	TBD	●	◐	◐	○	◐	◐	
94	Motorola Astro Transceiver, Portable; XTS 3000 Model 2	●	◐	●	TBD	○	TBD	TBD	●	◐	◐	○	◐	◐	
95	Motorola Astro Transceiver, Portable; XTS 3000 Model 3	●	◐	●	TBD	○	TBD	TBD	●	◐	◐	○	◐	◐	
96	Motorola Astro Transceiver, Portable; XTS 3000R Series Models 1, 2, & 3	●	◐	●	TBD	◐	TBD	TBD	●	◐	●	○	◐	◐	
108	Motorola Transceiver, Portable; MT 2000 VHF	●	○	●	TBD	◐	●	TBD	●	TBD	◐	○	◐	◐	
109	Motorola Transceiver, Portable; MTS 2000 Model I	●	◐	●	TBD	◐	●	TBD	○	TBD	◐	○	◐	◐	
110	Motorola Transceiver, Portable; MTS 2000 Model II	●	◐	●	TBD	◐	●	TBD	○	TBD	◐	○	◐	◐	

'TBD (to be determined) - there is currently no data available to support that selection factor.
'NA' - data field is not applicable for this piece of equipment.
See Table 4-12 for selection factor definitions.

23

Table 4-3. Portable communication equipment (conventional and trunked)
February 2001

Legend for symbols: ● = filled circle, ◑ = half-filled circle, ○ = empty circle, TBD = to be determined.

ID #	Equipment Name	Maximum Transmitter Power Output	Secure Communications Compatibility	Programmability	User Capability	Line of Sight	Power Requirements	Battery Life	Battery Locking Ability	Vehicular Adapter	Digital Communications Compatibility	Durability	Unit Cost	Operator Skill Level	Training Requirements
111	Motorola Transceiver, Portable; MTS 2000 Model III	●	◑	●	TBD	◑	●	TBD	○	TBD	◑	○	◑	◑	
112	Motorola Trunked Portable Radio; MTX 8000 Model B3	●	◑	●	TBD	◑	TBD	TBD	●	TBD	○	◑	◑	◑	
113	Motorola Trunked Portable Radio; MTX 8000 Model B5	●	◑	●	TBD	◑	TBD	TBD	●	TBD	○	○	◑	◑	
114	Motorola Trunked Portable Radio; MTX 8000/9000 Model B7	●	◑	●	TBD	◑	TBD	TBD	●	TBD	○	○	◑	◑	
145	Maxon UHF Transceiver, Portable; SP-150U	●	○	●	◑	○	●	●	○	○	◑	◑	◑	◑	
162	Vertex HX Series; HX482UT UHF Portable	●	○	●	TBD	○	◑	TBD	○	TBD	○	◑	◑	◑	
163	Vertex HX Series; HX580 Dual Protocol Hand Held	◑	○	●	TBD	◑	TBD	TBD	○	TBD	○	●	◑	◑	
164	Vertex VX Series; VX-210V (VHF Model)	●	◑	●	○	○	●	TBD	TBD	TBD	◑	●	●	●	
165	Vertex VX Series; VX-210U (UHF Model)	●	◑	●	○	○	◑	TBD	TBD	TBD	◑	●	●	●	
166	Vertex VX Series; VX-400V (VHF Model)	●	◑	●	○	○	●	TBD	TBD	TBD	◑	◑	●	●	

'TBD (to be determined) - there is currently no data available to support that selection factor.
'NA - data field is not applicable for this piece of equipment.
See Table 4-12 for selection factor definitions.

24

Table 4-3. Portable communication equipment (conventional and trunked)
February 2001

ID #	Equipment Name	Maximum Transmitter Power Output	Secure Communications Compatibility	Programmability	User Capability	Line of Sight	Power Requirements	Battery Life	Battery Locking Ability	Vehicular Adapter	Digital Communications Compatibility	Durability	Unit Cost	Operator Skill Level	Training Requirements
167	Vertex VX Series; VX-400U (UHF Model)	●	◐	●	○	○	◐	TBD	TBD	TBD	◐	◐	◐	●	●
168	Vertex VX Series; VX-500	●	◐	●	◐	○	◐	TBD	TBD	TBD	◐	◐	TBD	●	●
169	Vertex VX Series; VX-510LX (Low Band VHF)	●	◐	●	◐	○	●	TBD	TBD	TBD	◐	◐	◐	●	●
170	Vertex VX Series; VX-510V (VHF Model)	●	◐	●	○	○	●	TBD	TBD	TBD	◐	◐	◐	●	●
171	Vertex VX Series; VX-510U (UHF Model)	●	◐	●	○	○	●	TBD	TBD	TBD	◐	◐	◐	●	●

'TBD (to be determined) - there is currently no data available to support that selection factor.
'NA' - data field is not applicable for this piece of equipment.
See Table 4-12 for selection factor definitions.

25

Table 4-4. Portable communication equipment (conventional)
February 2001

ID #	Equipment Name	Maximum Transmitter Power Output	Secure Communications Compatibility	Programmability	User Capability	Line of Sight	Power Requirements	Battery Life	Battery Locking Ability	Vehicular Adapter	Digital Communications Compatibility	Durability	Unit Cost	Operator Skill Level
1	Communications-Applied Technology; AWIS Portable Radio	○	●	○	○	○	●	●	○	●	◐	○	●	●
3	Communications-Applied Technology; QB Series: QB-3S, QB-3S/IS/ QB-3R Portable Radios	○	○	NA	○	○	●	●	○	○	◐	○	●	●
6	EDACS™ M-RK™ Aegis™ Portable VHF, UHF, 800 MHz, M-RK I	●	●	●	●	○	●	●	●	●	●	○	◐	◐
7	EDACS™ M-RK™ Aegis™ Portable VHF, UHF, 800 MHz, M-RK II	●	●	●	●	○	●	●	●	●	●	○	◐	◐
8	EDACS™ M-RK™ Aegis™ Portable VHF, UHF, 800 MHz, M-RK II SCAN	●	●	●	●	○	●	●	●	●	●	○	◐	◐
19	ComNet Ericsson Panther Transceiver, Portable; Panther 400P	○	●	●	●	○	●	●	●	○	◐	●	◐	◐
20	ComNet Ericsson Panther Transceiver, Portable; Panther 500P	○	●	●	●	○	●	●	●	○	○	◐	●	●
21	ComNet Ericsson Panther Transceiver, Portable; Panther 600P	○	●	●	TBD	○	●	●	●	◐	◐	●	◐	◐
22	ComNet Ericsson Panther Transceiver, Portable; Panther 625P	○	●	●	TBD	○	●	●	●	◐	◐	◐	◐	◐
74	Kenwood Transceiver, Portable; TK-2100	◐	●	●	○	○	●	●	○	○	◐	●	●	●

'TBD (to be determined) - there is currently no data available to support that selection factor.
'NA' - data field is not applicable for this piece of equipment.
See Table 4-12 for selection factor definitions.

Table 4-4. Portable communication equipment (conventional)
February 2001

ID #	Equipment Name	Maximum Transmitter Power Output	Secure Communications Compatibility	Programmability	User Capability	Line of Sight	Power Requirements	Battery Life	Battery Locking Ability	Vehicular Adapter	Digital Communications Compatibility	Durability	Unit Cost	Operator Skill Level	Training Requirements
75	Kenwood Transceiver, Portable, TK-3100	◐	○	●	○	○	●	●	○	○	◐	●	●	●	
76	Kenwood Transceiver, Portable, TK-3101	◐	○	●	○	○	●	●	○	○	◐	●	●	●	
77	Kenwood VHF FM Transceivers, TK-290	●	◐	●	○	○	●	●	●	◐	◐	◐	◐	◐	
78	Kenwood UHF FM Transceivers, TK-390	●	◐	●	○	○	●	●	●	◐	◐	◐	◐	◐	
105	Motorola Transceiver, Portable, VISAR	●	○	●	TBD	◐	◐	TBD	○	TBD	◐	○	◐	◐	
106	Motorola Transceiver, Portable, HT 1000	●	○	●	TBD	◐	●	TBD	TBD	TBD	◐	○	◐	◐	
107	Motorola Transceiver, Portable, JT 1000	●	○	●	TBD	◐	TBD	TBD	●	TBD	○	○	◐	◐	
118	Racal Transceiver, Portable; MBITR (Multiband Inter/Intra Team Radio)	●	●	●	●	◐	●	●	●	●	●	○	◐	◐	
119	Racal Transceiver, Portable; MSHR (Miniature Secure Handheld Radio)	●	●	●	●	◐	◐	●	●	●	●	○	◐	◐	
120	Racal Transceiver, Portable; 20 Meter MSHR	●	●	●	●	◐	◐	●	●	●	●	○	◐	◐	

'TBD (to be determined) - there is currently no data available to support that selection factor.
'NA' - data field is not applicable for this piece of equipment.
See Table 4-12 for selection factor definitions.

Table 4-4. Portable communication equipment (conventional)
February 2001

ID #	Equipment Name	Maximum Transmitter Power Output	Secure Communications Compatibility	Programmability	User Capability	Line of Sight	Power Requirements	Battery Life	Battery Locking Ability	Vehicular Adapter	Digital Communications Compatibility	Durability	Unit Cost	Operator Skill Level	Training Requirements
121	Racal Transceiver, Portable; Racal 25	●	●	●	●	◐	●	●	TBD	●	●	○	◐	◐	
125	BK Synthesized FM E Series DES EPH 599, EPU 499 and EPV 499 Models	●	●	●	TBD	○	TBD	TBD	○	TBD	◐	○	◐	◐	
126	BK Synthesized FM Portable Radio; E Series, EPH 51 and 52 Models	●	○	●	TBD	○	TBD	TBD	○	TBD	◐	○	◐	◐	
127	BK Synthesized FM Portable Radio; E Series, EPI 510 Models	●	○	●	TBD	○	TBD	TBD	○	TBD	◐	○	◐	◐	
128	BK Synthesized FM Portable Radio; E Series, EPU & EPV 414 and 499 Models	●	○	●	TBD	○	TBD	TBD	○	TBD	◐	○	◐	◐	
130	BK Radio FM Transceiver, Portable; G Series, GPH Models	●	○	●	TBD	○	●	TBD	TBD	TBD	○	○	◐	◐	
133	Relm Portable Radios; MPU08 (UHF)	●	○	●	TBD	○	TBD	TBD	○	TBD	○	●	●	●	
134	Relm Portable Radios; MPU32 (UHF)	●	○	●	TBD	○	TBD	TBD	○	TBD	○	●	◐	◐	
135	Relm Portable Radios; MPV32 (VHF)	●	○	●	TBD	○	TBD	TBD	○	TBD	○	●	◐	◐	
141	Maxon Vhf/UHF Transceiver, Portable; SP-120	◐	◐	●	○	○	●	●	○	○	◐	●	◐	◐	

'TBD (to be determined) - there is currently no data available to support that selection factor.
'NA' - data field is not applicable for this piece of equipment.
See Table 4-12 for selection factor definitions.

Table 4-4. Portable communication equipment (conventional)
February 2001

Legend: ● = full, ◐ = half, ○ = empty, TBD = to be determined

ID #	Equipment Name	Maximum Transmitter Power Output	Secure Communications Compatibility	Programmability	User Capability	Line of Sight	Power Requirements	Battery Life	Battery Locking Ability	Vehicular Adapter	Digital Communications Compatibility	Durability	Unit Cost	Operator Skill Level	Training Requirements
142	Maxon VHF/UHF Transceiver, Portable; SP-130/SP-140	●	◐	●	◐	○	●	●	○	○	◐	●	◐	◐	
143	Maxon VHF/UHF Transceiver, Portable; SP-200	●	◐	●	◐	○	●	●	○	○	◐	◐	◐	◐	
144	Maxon VHF/UHF Transceiver, Portable; SP-300	●	◐	●	◐	○	●	●	○	○	◐	●	◐	◐	
146	Vertex Dual Band (VHF & UHF) Transceiver, Portable; FTH-2070	●	◐	●	○	○	●	TBD	○	TBD	◐	○	●	●	
152	Vertex VX Series; VX-10V (VHF Model)	●	◐	●	○	○	●	TBD	○	TBD	TBD	◐	●	●	
153	Vertex VX Series; VX-10U (UHF Model)	●	◐	●	○	○	◐	TBD	○	TBD	TBD	◐	●	●	
154	Vertex VX Series; VX-300	●	○	●	◐	◐	●	TBD	○	◐	◐	◐	●	●	
155	Vertex HX Series; HX120 UHF Portable	◐	○	●	●	○	●	TBD	TBD	TBD	TBD	●	●	●	
156	Vertex HX Series; HX120 VHF Portable	◐	○	●	●	○	●	TBD	TBD	TBD	TBD	●	●	●	
157	Vertex HX Series; HX140 VHF Portable	●	◐	●	TBD	○	TBD	TBD	TBD	TBD	◐	●	●	●	

TBD (to be determined) - there is currently no data available to support that selection factor.
NA - data field is not applicable for this piece of equipment.
See Table 4-12 for selection factor definitions.

Table 4-4. Portable communication equipment (conventional)
February 2001

ID #	Equipment Name	Maximum Transmitter Power Output	Secure Communications Compatibility	Programmability	User Capability	Line of Sight	Power Requirements	Battery Life	Battery Locking Ability	Vehicular Adapter	Digital Communications Compatibility	Durability	Unit Cost	Operator Skill Level	Training Requirements
158	Vertex HX Series; HX381 VHF Portable	●	◐	●	TBD	◔	TBD	TBD	TBD	TBD	◐	◐	●	●	
159	Vertex HX Series; HX381 UHF Portable	●	◐	●	TBD	◔	TBD	TBD	TBD	TBD	◐	◐	●	●	
160	Vertex HX Series; HX240 VHF Portable	●	○	●	TBD	◔	●	TBD	○	TBD	◐	●	◐	◐	
161	Vertex HX Series; HX240 UHF Portable	●	○	●	TBD	◔	●	TBD	○	TBD	◐	●	◐	◐	

'TBD (to be determined) - there is currently no data available to support that selection factor.
'NA' - data field is not applicable for this piece of equipment.
See Table 4-12 for selection factor definitions.

Table 4-5. Portable communication equipment (trunked)
February 2001

ID #	Equipment Name	Maximum Transmitter Power Output	Secure Communications Compatibility	Programmability	User Capability	Line of Sight	Power Requirements	Battery Life	Battery Locking Ability	Vehicular Adapter	Digital Communications Compatibility	Durability	Unit Cost	Operator Skill Level	Training Requirements
83	Kenwood 800/900 MHz FM Transceiver, TK-481	◐	◐	●	●	○	●	●	●	◐	◐	◐	◐	◐	

'TBD' (to be determined) - there is currently no data available to support that selection factor.
'NA' - data field is not applicable for this piece of equipment.
See Table 4-12 for selection factor definitions.

31

Table 4-6. Mobile communication equipment (conventional and trunked)
February 2001

ID #	Equipment Name	Maximum Transmitter Power Output	Secure Communications Compatibility	Programmability	User Capability	Line of Sight	Power Requirements	Battery Life	Battery Locking Ability	Vehicular Adapter	Digital Communications Compatibility	Durability	Unit Cost	Operator Skill Level	Training Requirements
15	ComNet Ericsson Orion Mobile Radio	●	●	●	●	●	NA	NA	NA	◐	◐	○	◐	◐	
25	ProVoice™ Orion™ Mobile 800 MHz	●	●	●	◐	●	NA	NA	NA	●	●	○	◐	◐	
37	EF Johnson Transceiver; 531x VHF	●	●	●	◐	●	NA	NA	NA	TBD	TBD	TBD	◐	◐	
38	EF Johnson Transceiver; 538x-800 MHz	●	●	●	◐	●	NA	NA	NA	TBD	TBD	TBD	◐	◐	
45	Icom VHF Mobile Transceiver; IC-F1020	●	○	●	●	●	NA	NA	NA	○	◐	◐	●	●	
46	Icom UHF Mobile Transceiver; IC-F2020	●	○	●	●	●	NA	NA	NA	○	◐	◐	●	●	
47	Icom VHF Mobile Transceiver; IC-F320/ IC-F420	●	○	●	●	●	NA	NA	NA	○	◐	●	●	●	
48	Icom UHF Mobile Transceiver; IC-F320S/ IC-F420S	●	◐	●	●	●	NA	NA	NA	○	◐	●	●	●	
59	Kenwood Compact Synthesized FM Mobile Radio, TK-760G	●	◐	●	●	●	NA	NA	NA	◐	◐	●	◐	○	
60	Kenwood Compact Synthesized FM Mobile Radio, TK-860G	●	◐	●	●	●	NA	NA	NA	◐	◐	◐	◐	○	

'TBD' (to be determined) - there is currently no data available to support that selection factor.
'NA' - data field is not applicable for this piece of equipment.
See Table 4-12 for selection factor definitions.

32

Table 4-6. Mobile communication equipment (conventional and trunked)
February 2001

ID #	Equipment Name	Maximum Transmitter Power Output	Secure Communications Compatibility	Programmability	User Capability	Line of Sight	Power Requirements	Battery Life	Battery Locking Ability	Vehicular Adapter	Digital Communications Compatibility	Durability	Unit Cost	Operator Skill Level	Training Requirements
61	Kenwood Compact Synthesized FM Mobile Radio; TK-762G	●	◐	●	●	●	NA	NA	NA	◐	◐	●	◐	◐	
62	Kenwood Compact Synthesized FM Mobile Radio; TK-862G	●	◐	●	●	●	NA	NA	NA	◐	◐	●	◐	◐	
72	Kenwood VHF/UHF Mobile Radio; TK-780	●	◐	●	●	●	NA	NA	NA	◐	◐	◐	◐	◐	
73	Kenwood VHF/UHF Mobile Radio; TK-880	●	◐	●	●	●	NA	NA	NA	◐	◐	◐	◐	◐	
85	Kenwood Trunked Compact Mobile Radio; TK-980	●	◐	●	◐	●	NA	NA	NA	◐	◐	◐	◐	◐	
86	Kenwood Trunked Compact Mobile Radio; TK-81	●	◐	●	◐	●	NA	NA	NA	◐	◐	◐	◐	◐	
97	Motorola Dual Mode Mobile; MCS 2000 Mobile Model II	●	◐	◐	●	●	NA	NA	NA	○	○	○	◐	◐	
98	Motorola Dual Mode Mobile; MCS 2000 Mobile Model II	●	◐	◐	●	●	NA	NA	NA	TBD	○	◐	◐	◐	
99	Motorola Dual Mode Mobile; MCS 2000 Mobile Model III	●	◐	◐	●	●	NA	NA	NA	TBD	○	○	◐	◐	
100	Motorola Transceiver, Astro Digital Spectra W3	●	◐	◐	●	●	NA	NA	NA	●	○	○	◐	◐	

'TBD' (to be determined) - there is currently no data available to support that selection factor.
'NA' - data field is not applicable for this piece of equipment
See Table 4-12 for selection factor definitions.

33

Table 4-6. Mobile communication equipment (conventional and trunked)
February 2001

ID #	Equipment Name	Maximum Transmitter Power Output	Secure Communications Compatibility	Programmability	User Capability	Line of Sight	Power Requirements	Battery Life	Battery Locking Ability	Vehicular Adapter	Digital Communications Compatibility	Durability	Unit Cost	Operator Skill Level	Training Requirements
101	Motorola Transceiver, Astro Spectra W4	●	◐	●	◐	●	NA	NA	NA	TBD	○	○	◐	◐	
102	Motorola Transceiver, Astro Spectra W5	●	◐	●	◐	●	NA	NA	NA	◐	○	○	◐	◐	
103	Motorola Transceiver, Astro Spectra W7	●	◐	●	◐	●	NA	NA	NA	◐	○	○	◐	◐	
104	Motorola Transceiver, Astro Spectra W9	●	◐	●	◐	●	NA	NA	NA	◐	○	○	◐	◐	
147	Vertex FTL Series; FTL-1011 (VHF LowBand)	●	◐	●	◐	●	NA	NA	NA	◐	◐	TBD	◐	◐	
148	Vertex FTL Series; FTL-1011H (VHF LowBand HiPower)	●	◐	●	◐	●	NA	NA	NA	◐	◐	TBD	◐	◐	
149	Vertex FTL Series; FTL-2011 (VHF Highband)	●	◐	●	◐	●	NA	NA	NA	◐	◐	TBD	◐	◐	
150	Vertex FTL Series; FTL-7011 (UHF)	●	◐	●	◐	●	NA	NA	NA	◐	◐	TBD	◐	◐	
172	Vertex VX Series; VX-2000V Mobile Radio (VHF)	●	◐	●	◐	●	NA	NA	NA	◐	◐	TBD	◐	◐	
173	Vertex VX Series; VX-2000U Mobile Radio (UHF)	●	◐	●	◐	●	NA	NA	NA	○	◐	TBD	◐	◐	

TBD (to be determined) - there is currently no data available to support that selection factor.
NA - data field is not applicable for this piece of equipment.
See Table 4-12 for selection factor definitions.

Table 4-6. Mobile communication equipment (conventional and trunked)
February 2001

ID #	Equipment Name	Maximum Transmitter Power Output	Secure Communications Compatibility	Programmability	User Capability	Line of Sight	Power Requirements	Battery Life	Battery Locking Ability	Vehicular Adapter	Digital Communications Compatibility	Durability	Unit Cost	Operator Skill Level	Training Requirements
174	Vertex VX Series; VX-3000L (VHF Lowband)	●	○	●	◑	●	NA	NA	NA	◑	◑	TBD	◑	◑	
175	Vertex VX Series; VX-3000V (VHF)	●	○	●	◑	●	NA	NA	NA	◑	◑	TBD	◑	◑	
176	Vertex VX Series; VX-3000U (UHF)	●	○	●	◑	●	NA	NA	NA	◑	◑	TBD	◑	◑	

'TBD (to be determined) - there is currently no data available to support that selection factor.
'NA' - data field is not applicable for this piece of equipment.
See Table 4-12 for selection factor definitions.

Table 4-7. Mobile communication equipment (conventional)
February 2001

ID #	Equipment Name	Maximum Transmitter Power Output	Secure Communications Compatibility	Programmability	User Capability	Line of Sight	Power Requirements	Battery Life	Battery Locking Ability	Vehicular Adapter	Digital Communications Compatibility	Durability	Unit Cost	Operator Skill Level	Training Requirements
17	ComNet Ericsson Panther Transceiver, Mobile Panther 400M	●	◐	●	●	●	NA	NA	NA	○	◐	●	◐	◐	
18	ComNet Ericsson Panther Transceiver, Mobile Panther 600M	●	◐	●	●	●	NA	NA	NA	○	◐	◐	◐	◐	
63	Kenwood Compact Synthesized FM Mobile Radio; TK-760H	●	●	●	●	●	NA	NA	NA	◐	◐	◐	◐	◐	
64	Kenwood Compact Synthesized FM Mobile Radio; TK-860H	●	●	●	●	●	NA	NA	NA	◐	◐	◐	◐	◐	
65	Kenwood Compact Synthesized FM Mobile Radio; TK-762H	●	●	●	●	●	NA	NA	NA	◐	◐	●	◐	◐	
66	Kenwood Compact Synthesized FM Mobile Radio; TK-862H	●	●	●	●	●	NA	NA	NA	◐	◐	●	◐	◐	
67	Kenwood Public Safety Mobile FM Radios; TK-690H	●	◐	●	●	●	NA	NA	NA	◐	◐	○	◐	◐	
68	Kenwood Public Safety Mobile FM Radios; TK-790	●	◐	●	●	●	NA	NA	NA	◐	◐	◐	◐	◐	
69	Kenwood Public Safety Mobile FM Radios; TK-790H	●	◐	●	●	●	NA	NA	NA	◐	◐	○	◐	◐	
70	Kenwood Public Safety Mobile FM Radios; TK-890	●	◐	●	●	●	NA	NA	NA	◐	◐	◐	◐	◐	

'TBD' (to be determined) - there is currently no data available to support that selection factor.
'NA' - data field is not applicable for this piece of equipment.
See Table 4-12 for selection factor definitions.

Table 4-7. Mobile communication equipment (conventional)
February 2001

ID #	Equipment Name	Maximum Transmitter Power Output	Secure Communications	Programmability	User Capability	Line of Sight	Power Requirements	Battery Life	Battery Locking Ability	Vehicular Adapter	Digital Communications Compatibility	Durability	Unit Cost	Operator Skill Level	Training Requirements
71	Kenwood Public Safety Mobile FM Radios; TK-890H	●	◐	●	●	●	NA	NA	NA	◐	◐	○	◐	◐	
123	BK Radio FM Transceiver, EMH 599 2X	●	○	●	●	●	NA	NA	NA	TBD	◐	○	◐	◐	
124	BK Synthesized FM Mobile Radio; EMV	●	TBD	●	●	●	NA	NA	NA	TBD	◐	○	◐	◐	
131	BK Radio Airborne Transceiver, KFM 985	●	○	●	●	●	NA	NA	NA	TBD	◐	TBD	◐	◐	
132	Relm Mobile Radio; 256NB	●	○	●	●	●	NA	NA	NA	TBD	TBD	TBD	◐	◐	
136	Relm Mobile Radios; SMV2516	●	○	●	●	●	NA	NA	NA	TBD	◐	◐	◐	◐	
137	Relm Mobile Radios; SMV4016	●	○	●	●	●	NA	NA	NA	TBD	◐	◐	◐	◐	
139	Maxon Scanning Transceiver, SM-2000 Series	●	◐	●	●	●	NA	NA	NA	○	◐	●	◐	◐	
140	Maxon Scanning Transceiver, SM-4000 Series	●	○	●	●	●	NA	NA	NA	○	◐	◐	◐	◐	

'TBD' (to be determined) - there is currently no data available to support that selection factor.
'NA' - data field is not applicable for this piece of equipment.
See Table 4-12 for selection factor definitions.

Table 4-8. Mobile communication equipment (trunked)
February 2001

ID #	Equipment Name	Maximum Transmitter Power Output	Secure Communications Compatibility	Programmability	User Capability	Line of Sight	Power Requirements	Battery Life	Battery Locking Ability	Vehicular Adapter	Digital Communications Compatibility	Durability	Unit Cost	Operator Skill Level	Training Requirements
79	Kenwood Trunked Mobile Radio, TK-980 NSPAC	●	◐	●	●	◐	●	NA	NA	◐	◐	◐	◐	◐	
151	Vertex GX4800UT Mobile Transceiver	●	○	●	◐	●	●	NA	NA	TBD	◐	TBD	◐	◐	

'TBD' (to be determined) - there is currently no data available to support that selection factor.
'NA' - data field is not applicable for this piece of equipment.
See Table 4-12 for selection factor definitions.

38

Table 4-9. Repeaters communication equipment
February 2001

ID #	Equipment Name	Technology	Maximum Transmitter Power Output	Secure Communications Compatibility	Programmability	User Capability	Line of Sight	Power Requirements	Digital Communications Compatibility	Durability	Unit Cost	Operator Skill Level	Training Requirements
2	Communications-Applied Technology: DWIS Portable Repeater System	Conventional or Trunking, Digital DSSS TDMA	○	●	○	○	◐	●	◐	○	●	●	
4	Communications-Applied Technology; QB Series Repeater: Portable Repeater Systems	Conventional	○	○	NA	○	◐	○	◐	○	●	◐	
14	ComNet Ericsson Repeater, MASTR III	Conventional or Trunking	NA	●	●	NA	●	●	●	○	◐	◐	
16	ComNet Ericsson Repeater, Orion Transportable Repeater	Conventional or Trunking	NA	◐	●	NA	●	●	●	○	◐	◐	
27	EF Johnson Auris Repeater; RS-5601 VHF; Single Channel	Conventional Digital	NA	●	●	NA	●	●	○	○	◐	◐	
28	EF Johnson Auris Digital Repeater, RS-5611 VHF, Dual Channel	Conventional Digital	NA	●	●	NA	●	●	○	○	◐	◐	
31	EF Johnson Auris Repeater; RS-5604 (Single Channel)/5614 (Dual Channel) UHF	Conventional	NA	●	●	NA	●	●	○	○	◐	◐	
53	Modular Interconnect System, ACU-1000	Conventional Modular Interconnect Communications Interoperability System	NA	●	◐	NA	●	◐	◐	TBD	TBD	TBD	
54	Transportable Radio Interconnect System, TRP-1000	Trunking/ Conventional Transportable Interconnect/ Communications Interoperability System	NA	●	◐	NA	●	◐	◐	TBD	TBD	TBD	

'TBD (to be determined)- there is currently no data available to support that selection factor.
'NA' - data field is not applicable for this piece of equipment
See Table 4-12 for selection factor definitions.

Table 4-9. Repeaters communication equipment
February 2001

ID #	Equipment Name		Maximum Transmitter Power Output	Secure Communications Compatibility	Programmability	User Capability	Line of Sight	Power Requirements	Digital Communications Compatibility	Durability	Unit Cost	Operator Skill Level	Training Requirements
88	Kenwood VHF/UHF Repeater, TKR-720	Conventional Desktop Repeater	NA	◐	●	NA	◐	○	○	○	◐	◐	◐
89	Kenwood UHF Repeater, TKR-820	Conventional Desktop Repeater	NA	◐	●	NA	◐	○	○	○	◐	◐	◐
117	Motorola Portable Repeater, Portable Repeater 2	Conventional	NA	●	●	NA	●	TBD	○	○	◐	◐	◐
129	BK Repeater; ERU Series	Conventional	NA	○	●	NA	●	○	◐	TBD	○	○	○
138	Maxon VHF/UHF RF Link Module; SD-125	Link Conventional RF Link (Repeater) Module	NA	◐	NA	NA	●	◐	○	●	●	●	◐
177	Vertex Repeaters; VXR-1000 (VHF)	Conventional Mobile Repeaters	NA	●	●	NA	●	TBD	◐	◐	○	○	○
178	Vertex Repeaters; VXR-1000 (UHF)	Conventional Mobile Repeater	NA	●	●	NA	●	TBD	◐	◐	○	○	○
179	Vertex Repeaters; VXR-5000 (VHF)	Trunking Mobile Repeater	NA	○	●	NA	◐	TBD	◐	TBD	○	○	○

'TBD (to be determined) - there is currently no data available to support that selection factor.
'NA' - data field is not applicable for this piece of equipment.
See Table 4-12 for selection factor definitions.

40

Table 4-10. Base station communication equipment
February 2001

ID #	Equipment Name	Maximum Transmitter Power Output	Secure Communications Compatibility	Programmability	User Capability	Line of Sight	Power Requirements	Digital Communications Compatibility	Durability	Unit Cost	Operator Skill Level	Training Requirements
26	EF Johnson Auris Digital Base Station; RS-5601 VHF; Single Channel — Conventional Digital Base Station	NA	○	●	NA	●	●	●	○	○	◑	
29	EF Johnson Auris Digital Base Station; RS-5611 VHF; Dual Channel — Conventional Digital Base Station	NA	○	●	NA	●	●	●	○	○	◑	
87	Kenwood VHF Base Tranceiver; TKB-720 — Conventional Base Radio	NA	◑	●	◑	◑	○	○	○	○	◑	
122	BK Base Station; EBU Series — Conventional Base Station	NA	○	●	NA	●	TBD	◑	○	TBD	○	

'TBD' (to be determined) - there is currently no data available to support that selection factor.
'NA' - data field is not applicable for this piece of equipment.
See Table 4-12 for selection factor definitions.

Table 4-11. Base station and/or repeater communication equipment
February 2001

ID #	Equipment Name	Maximum Transmitter Power Output	Secure Communications Compatibility	Programmability	User Capability	Line of Sight	Power Requirements	Digital Communications Compatibility	Durability	Unit Cost	Operator Skill Level	Training Requirements
24	ProVoice™ MASTR™ III Base Station 800 MHz	Mobile Base Station or Repeater (Trunking is the primary operating mode)	NA	●	●	NA	●	●	●	○	◐	◐	
30	EF Johnson Auris Digital Repeater/Basestation; RS-5604 (Single Channel)/5614 (Dual Channel) UHF	Digital Base Station (Conventional)	NA	●	●	NA	●	●	○	○	◐	◐	
115	Motorola Station/Repeater; QUANTAR	Functions as a Base Station or Repeater (Conventional or Trunking)	NA	●	●	NA	●	◐	○	○	◐	◐	
116	Motorola Station/Repeater; QUANTRO	Base Station/Repeater (Conventional/Trunking)	NA	●	●	NA	●	◐	○	○	◐	◐	
180	Vertex Repeaters or Base Station; VXR-5000 (UHF)	Mobile Base Station or Repeater (Conventional; Trunking Capable with Optional Accessory Board)	NA	●	●	NA	●	TBD	NA	TBD	○	○	
181	Vertex Repeater or Base Station; VXR-7000 (VHF)	Mobile Base Station or Repeater (Conventional; Optional VX-Trunk Operation)	NA	●	●	NA	●	TBD	NA	TBD	○	○	

'TBD (to be determined) - there is currently no data available to support that selection factor.
'NA' - data field is not applicable for this piece of equipment.
See Table 4-12 for selection factor definitions.

Table 4-12. Selection factor key for communication equipment
February 2001

Symbol	Maximum Transmitter Power Output	Secure Communications Compatibility	Programmability	User Capability	Line of Sight	Power Requirements (Portable)	Power Requirements (Mobile and Repeater)	Battery Life (Portable)	Battery Locking Ability (Portable)	Vehicular Adapter (Portable)	Digital Communications Compatibility	Durability	Unit Cost	Operator Skill Level	Training Requirements (Portable)	Training Requirements (Mobile and Repeater)
●	Power output of 3 W to 5 W	Capable of secure transmissions without an accessory	Can be programmed/reprogrammed by authorized personnel	Unlimited capability	Transmission can travel 10 miles or more	Operates off battery pack, external dc, or ac adapter	Uses 12 V dc to 15 V dc	Equal to or greater than 8 h	Battery securely locked into place on the radio and cannot be dislodged by bumping or dropping	Has vehicle adapter (with built-in amplifier) that connects to vehicle's electrical system and external antenna	Capable of digital transmissions without an adaptor	Designed for rugged use and is submersible in water	Less than or equal to $500 per unit	No special skills or training required	No special training required	No special training required
◐						Operates off battery pack or external dc adapter										
◑	Power output of more than 1.5 W but less than 3 W	Capable of secure transmissions with an accessory	Can be programmed/reprogrammed by vendor only	Fixed capability	Transmission can travel 5 miles to 10 miles	Operates off battery pack or ac adapter	Uses 120/220 V ac	Greater than 4 h but less than 8 h			Capable of digital transmissions with an adaptor	Designed for rugged use but is not submersible in water	Greater than $500 but less than $1000 per unit	No special skills but some training required	Less than 60 min training required	Less than 8 h training required
○	Power output of less than 1.5 W	Not capable of secure transmissions	Can be programmed/reprogrammed by the end user	Restrictive capability	Transmission can travel less than 5 miles	Operates off battery pack only	Uses voltage other than standard 12 V dc to 15 V dc or 110/220 V ac	Less than 4 h	Battery not locked into place	Does not have optional vehicle adapter	Not capable of digital transmissions	Designed for standard use only	Greater than $1000 per unit	Technical background required to operate equipment	More than 60 min training required	More than 8 h training required

The gray cells designate that the symbol is not applicable for the selection factor.

43

APPENDIX A—RECOMMENDED QUESTIONS ON COMMUNICATION EQUIPMENT

APPENDIX A—RECOMMENDED QUESTIONS ON COMMUNICATION EQUIPMENT[5]

Buying detection, protection, decontamination, and communication equipment to respond to the threatened terrorist use of chemical or biological warfare agents may be new for public safety agencies. To help procurement officials obtain the best value for their domestic preparedness dollar, a series of questions was excerpted from a report titled: "Domestic Preparedness Program in Defense of Weapons of Mass Destruction Report on Communication Equipment" (see detailed reference in appendix B). These questions should assist officials in selecting products from the large number in the present day marketplace. Requesting vendors to provide written responses to specific questions may also be helpful in the decision process.

Note: The included question lists are meant as starting points only. The consumer should add any questions pertinent to a particular application.

Portable Radio Accessories

1. Can I use the accessory with or without a facemask?
2. Can I use the accessory with an encapsulated suit?
3. What radios are compatible with the unit?
4. How does the equipment function in high noise (a lot of electrical or environmental interference) surroundings?
5. Does the equipment require batteries? How many? What type? Battery life?
6. Is the equipment waterproof?
7. Is the equipment spark proof, intrinsically safe, or explosion proof?
8. Is the product voice activated? Push-to-talk (PTT)? Both? How big is the PTT switch?
9. Can the PTT be activated through a suit? How tactile is the switch?
10. What receiver options are available?
11. Can the unit be decontaminated?
12. Does other protective equipment affect the clarity of communication?
13. Will communication capability be affected by the removal or addition of any personal protective equipment (PPE)?
14. Is the product ruggedly constructed? What is the warranty period?
15. Who uses the product now? Where? For what application?
16. How much does a complete unit with radio interface cable cost?
17. What is the cost of ownership over time? (i.e., batteries, additional components, etc.)

Portable Radio Capabilities

1. Is voice communication continuous?
2. What is the level of intrinsic safety?
3. What materials are used in the construction of the equipment?
4. Is the equipment waterproof? Immersion proof?
5. What is the power source? Batteries (type)? Other?

---

[5] The information in Appendix A was provided by the National Domestic Preparedness Office (NDPO) in coordination with the National Institute of Justice and Technical Support Working Group.

6.   What is the battery life? Is there a low battery warning?
7.   Can it be used while wearing breathing apparatus?
8.   What kind of accessories are available for the equipment?
9.   Are system components and accessories interchangeable?
10.   How quickly can the equipment be deployed?
11.   Is the equipment shielded against RF or electromagnetic interference?
12.   How easy is it to use? How much training is required?
13.   How many people can be on the communication system at once?
14.   What type of warranty does it come with?
15.   Is the equipment built to a quality standard? What standard?

APPENDIX B—REFERENCES

APPENDIX B—REFERENCES

1. Andy Ibbetson, *Domestic Preparedness Program in Defense of Weapons of Mass Destruction Report on Communication Equipment*, CON-SPACE Communication Inc., October 26, 1999.

APPENDIX C—EQUIPMENT SAFETY

APPENDIX C—EQUIPMENT SAFETY[6]

Types of Electrical Equipment

Some examples of commonly used electrical equipment by rescuers in hazardous locations are two-way radios, hard-line and sound powered communication systems, gas detectors PASS devices, pagers, and ventilation equipment. However, electrical equipment, as defined by Factory Mutual Research in their Approval Standard 3600, is "All items applied as a whole or in part for the utilization of electrical energy. These include, among others, items for the generation, transmission, storage, measurement, regulation, conversion, and consumption of electrical energy and items for telecommunications."

Equipment Safety

When selecting electrically powered communication equipment for use in a hazardous or potentially hazardous environment, it is important to choose equipment that has been designed and approved to be spark proof, explosion proof, or intrinsically safe. The classifications for hazardous locations are in the National Electrical Code (NFPA 70).

The following is an abbreviated list of the different classifications and what they mean. If there is any doubt about the approval rating on a particular piece of equipment, check the label. In North America, all intrinsically safe or explosion proof equipment has to carry a label that lists the hazardous location or hazardous locations for which it has been tested and approved. If the hazardous location information is not on the label, it is not approved for that location and, if there is no label, the equipment is not approved. If the physical size of the equipment prohibits a listing of approved locations, as a minimum requirement, the equipment will have the mark of the Nationally Recognized Test Laboratory (NTRL) that did the testing. If there is any question about the approval status for a piece of electrical equipment, request a copy of the certification record or approval agreement from the equipment manufacturer or distributor and keep it on file for future reference.

---

[6] Appendix C has been copied in its entirety from "Report on Communication Equipment, (Domestic Preparedness Program in Defense of Weapons of Mass Destruction)." This is a circulated document prepared by Andy Ibbetson, CON-SPACE Communication Inc., October 26, 1999.

National Electrical Code (NEC) Classifications for Hazardous Locations

Class I	Locations where there is a danger of explosion due to flammable gases or vapors present in quantities sufficient to produce explosive or ignitable mixtures.
Class II	Locations where there is a danger of explosion due to the presence of combustible or electrically conductive dust.
Class III	Locations where there is a danger of explosion or flash fire due to the presence of easily ignitable fibers or flyings.
Classes are separated into Divisions 1 and 2	
Division 1	Locations where the gases, vapors, conductive dust, combustible dust, flyings and/or fibers are present in the air in potentially flammable concentrations continuously, frequently, or intermittently under normal operating conditions.
Division 2	Locations where the gases, vapors, conductive dust, combustible dust, flyings and/or fibers might become hazardous in the event of mechanical breakdown, accident, failure, or the abnormal operation of equipment.
Classes are further divided into Groups	
Class I	
Group A	Acetylene.
Group B	Butadiene, Hydrogen, Ethylene Oxide, Propylene Oxide, and Acrolien.
Group C	Acetaldehyde, Ethylene, and Ether Vapors.
Group D	Acetone, Ammonia, Benzene, Butane, Cyclopropane, Gasoline, Hexane, Methane, Methanol, Natural Gas, Naptha, and Propane.
Class II	
Group E	Combustible metal dust including aluminium, magnesium and their commercial alloys.
Group F	Combustible carbonaceous dusts including Carbon Black, coal, and charcoal.
Group G	Combustible dusts not listed in groups E or F including flour, grain, wood, and plastic.
Class III	No Groups.

Zones

The 1996 version of the National Electrical Code (NEC) included Article 505 – Class I, Zone 0, 1, and 2 Locations. Article 505 specifies an alternative hazardous location identification scheme for Class I environments. The Zone system does not replace the aforementioned classification system, but since Zones are common classifications elsewhere in the world, its inclusion in the NEC should be considered a step toward standardization of I.S. approval standards with other countries.

Special Note: NEC Article 500–3 states that if Article 505 is used, area classification, wiring, and equipment selection must be done under the supervision of a qualified Registered Professional Engineer.

Class 1 – Zones*	
Zone 0	Location in which ignitable concentrations of flammable gases and vapors are present either continuously or for long periods of time.
Zone 1	Location in which ignitable concentrations of flammable gases or vapors that are likely to exist under normal operating conditions or may exist frequently because of repair maintenance, leakage, or breakdown. Or the location is adjacent to a Class I, Zone 0 from which ignitable concentrations could be communicated, unless prevented by adequate positive pressure ventilation and safeguards are in place to prevent ventilation failure.
Zone 2	Location in which ignitable concentrations of flammable gases or vapors that are not likely to occur in normal operation and if they do occur will exist only for a short period of time. An area where liquids gases or vapors are normally confined in closed containers or systems that could escape due to an accidental rupture, breakdown, or abnormal operation of equipment. Or where the ignitable concentrations are normally prevented by positive mechanical ventilation but could become hazardous due to the failure or abnormal operation of the ventilation equipment. Or the location is adjacent to a Class I, Zone 1 from which ignitable concentrations could be communicated, unless prevented by adequate positive pressure ventilation and safeguards are in place to prevent ventilation failure.

Group Equivalents

Zone System	=	Current System
Class I, Group IIc	=	Class I, Groups A & B
Class I, Group IIb	=	Class I, Group C
Class I, Group IIa	=	Class I, Group D

*The above is an abbreviated version of the Zone/Group system and is for information purposes only. Refer to the NEC Article 505 for complete descriptions of Class I, Zones and Groups.

Examples of Classifications and Corresponding Rescue Sites

Note: Refer to the National Electrical Code Articles 500, 501, 502, 503, 505 for a complete description of Hazardous Area Classifications and Group descriptions including an alternative hazardous location identification scheme (Zone Classification System).

Class I, Divisions 1 & 2

Petroleum refineries, dry cleaning plants, petrochemical plants, hospitals, utilities, aircraft hangers, paint manufacturers, dip tanks containing flammable or combustible liquids, and spray finishing areas.

Class II, Divisions 1 & 2

Grain elevators, flour and feed mills, confectionery plants, fireworks manufacturing and storage, grain ships, areas for packaging and handling of pulverized sugar and cocoa, manufacturing and storage of magnesium or aluminium, spice grinding mills, and some coal handling plants.

Class III, Divisions 1 & 2

Wood working plants, textile mills, cotton gins, cottonseed mills, flax producing plants, knitting mills, and weaving mills.

NOTE: The above is an example only. Individual group classifications also apply to the above and were omitted for brevity. To determine Classifications for specific locations, consult with your safety officer.

ABOUT THE LAW ENFORCEMENT AND CORRECTIONS STANDARDS AND TESTING PROGRAM

The Law Enforcement and Corrections Standards and Testing Program is sponsored by the Office of Science and Technology of the National Institute of Justice (NIJ), U.S. Department of Justice. The program responds to the mandate of the Justice System Improvement Act of 1979, directed NIJ to encourage research and development to improve the criminal justice system and to disseminate the results to Federal, State, and local agencies.

The Law Enforcement and Corrections Standards and Testing Program is an applied research effort that determines the technological needs of justice system agencies, sets minimum performance standards for specific devices, tests commercially available equipment against those standards, and disseminates the standards and the test results to criminal justice agencies nationally and internationally.

The program operates through:

The *Law Enforcement and Corrections Technology Advisory Council* (LECTAC), consisting of nationally recognized criminal justice practitioners from Federal, State, and local agencies, which assesses technological needs and sets priorities for research programs and items to be evaluated and tested.

The *Office of Law Enforcement Standards* (OLES) at the National Institute of Standards and Technology, which develops voluntary national performance standards for compliance testing to ensure that individual items of equipment are suitable for use by criminal justice agencies. The standards are based upon laboratory testing and evaluation of representative samples of each item of equipment to determine the key attributes, develop test methods, and establish minimum performance requirements for each essential attribute. In addition to the highly technical standards, OLES also produces technical reports and user guidelines that explain in nontechnical terms the capabilities of available equipment.

The *National Law Enforcement and Corrections Technology Center* (NLECTC), operated by a grantee, which supervises a national compliance testing program conducted by independent laboratories. The standards developed by OLES serve as performance benchmarks against which commercial equipment is measured. The facilities, personnel, and testing capabilities of the independent laboratories are evaluated by OLES prior to testing each item of equipment, and OLES helps the NLECTC staff review and analyze data. Test results are published in Equipment Performance Reports designed to help justice system procurement officials make informed purchasing decisions.

Publications are available at no charge through the National Law Enforcement and Corrections Technology Center. Some documents are also available online through the Internet/World Wide Web. To request a document or additional information, call 800–248–2742 or 301–519–5060, or write:

National Law Enforcement and Corrections Technology Center
P.O. Box 1160
Rockville, MD 20849–1160
E-Mail: *asknlectc@nlectc.org*
World Wide Web address: *http://www.nlectc.org*

This document is not intended to create, does not create, and may not be relied upon to create any rights, substantive or procedural, enforceable at law by any party in any matter civil or criminal.

Opinions or points of view expressed in this document represent a consensus of the authors and do not represent the official position or policies of the U.S. Department of Justice. The products and manufacturers discussed in this document are presented for informational purposes only and do not constitute product approval or endorsement by the U.S. Department of Justice.